Prevailing Purpose

Beauty in the Breaking

k. buehler

Prevailing Purpose: Beauty in the Breaking
© 2025 Krista Tedrow, writing as k. buehler
All rights reserved.

No part of this publication may be reproduced, distributed, or transmitted in any form or by any means—electronic, mechanical, photocopying, recording, or otherwise—without the prior written permission of the author, except in the case of brief quotations embodied in critical reviews and articles.

This publication may not be used or reproduced in any manner, in whole or in part, for the purpose of training artificial intelligence systems or technologies. Any use of the content in datasets or model training without express written permission is strictly prohibited.

For permissions or inquiries, please contact:
tedrow.krista@gmail.com

Published in Ottumwa, Iowa, United States by: NOW LLC
Library of Congress Cataloging-in-Publication Data
Names: buehler, k. (Krista Tedrow), author.
Title: Prevailing Purpose: Beauty in the Breaking / by k. buehler.
Description: First edition. | United States: NOW LLC, 2025.
Identifiers: LCCN 2025908148 (print) | ISBN 979-8-9907284-4-8 (Paperback)
Printed in the United States of America
First Edition

Dedication

for the ones who broke and kept loving.
for the ones who stayed when they could've shut down.
for the ones who cracked open instead of closing off.
this is for you.

for the seekers, the survivors, the sacredly sensitive.
for the ones who kept showing up with trembling hands and tender hope.
for the ones who dared to believe that purpose could still rise from the places that tried to bury them.

this is for my daughter,
whose laughter rewired my heart,
whose presence made me a child again,
and whose eyes remind me every day—
this life is worth healing for.

for my partner, who weathers the storms,
not always knowing the way.

for the people who saw me when I forgot how to see myself.

and to anyone holding pieces,
wondering if they'll ever fit—
this book is proof
that you can.
a reminder that you are already whole
even in the breaking.

for the little girl I used to be—
this one's for you.
we made it.

Acknowledgements

There is no such thing as becoming alone. And this book— this living, breathing collection of process and promise—was not created in isolation. It was carried. Held. Witnessed.

To Debbie—you have been with me through all the years and all the tears. You are more than family. You are a steady grace. A soft landing. A fierce protector and the kind of grandmother every child dreams of. Amelia and I are endlessly blessed by your love. Thank you for showing up in ways words will never be able to capture.

To Jim—thank you for seeing me long before this book was born. For holding space. For reading the first draft and offering both insight and heart. For writing the foreward with the same intentionality and presence you've offered me over the years. Your belief in me—and your willingness to share my story with your world—means more than you know.

To Brad—for your thoughtful edits, your careful eyes, and your unwavering support. Thank you for walking with me through the messy middle. For staying when it wasn't polished. For honoring the vision and believing in the voice behind it.

To my inner circle of beta readers—you know who

you are. Your reflections helped me feel the resonance and refine the rhythm. Thank you for reading with your hearts wide open.

To Aaron—your love and friendship has shaped this journey in more ways than I can name.

And to me—yes, you. The one who sat down to write even when the words hurt. The one who kept showing up to the page with trembling hands and a flicker of faith. The one who dared to believe this story mattered. You didn't give up. You didn't shrink. You wrote it down, even when your voice shook. You turned your pain into poetry. Your becoming into a book. And that is no small thing.

Thank you to everyone who held a part of this story. This book carries your fingerprints and your love between every line.

We did this. Together.

Map of Becoming

Foreward	1
Note From Author	3
Introduction	5
The Cocoon of Crisis	7
Carried Then Cut Free	17
The Sacred Scattering	29
The Remembering	43
The Reclamation	57
The Space Between Us	69
Finding Me	81
The Cloak	93
Curious You PhD In Me	109
The Promise	123
Healing Resources	135

Foreword

I have been fortunate throughout my life to work with and come into contact with many amazing people — Presidents, CEOs, Congressman, Senators and entrepreneurs. This will surprise the author of *Prevailing Purpose*, but I would place her in the top 5% of authentic, full-circle people that I know.

In every life, there are stories that remain untold or hidden beneath layers of shame, fear and silence. This rendering is such a piece. The author invites us into her past where the shadows of a dark childhood loom large. She allows us to journey with her as she navigates the tumultuous waters of trauma, seeking solace and ultimately, understanding. It's not a linear path, nor is it simple. But she writes in a way that will touch you and is simple to understand while providing great introspective points to ponder.

I am not a voracious reader of poetry. The author begins each chapter with a brief self-disclosing poem, that served to make my thought process more vulnerable and made the ensuing chapters more meaningful.

The narrative is compelling and authentic. The author lays bare painful truths and experiences that offer a mirror through which the reader can confront their own hidden wounds or better understand others in their journey. This memoir serves as a reminder that while the past may shape us, it does not define us. The strength to rise, to rebuild and to embrace the person we are becoming resides within us all.

As you read about the author's journey, I believe you may be inspired to affect your own journey. *Prevailing Purpose* is truly a story for anyone who has ever felt lost, broken or unheard and is a testament to the enduring power of the human spirit to overcome and heal.

Most Sincerely,
Jim Lindenmayer, PhD
Lifelong Educator

Note From The Author

Thank you for holding this book. For picking it up. For letting it find its way into your hands, or your heart, through a whisper, a click, a recommendation, or maybe... divine timing.

However it got here, I'm grateful.

A gentle note before you turn the page: Within these chapters (specifically *The Remembering)* I speak honestly about my experiences—including childhood trauma, sexual abuse, and emotional pain. While I do not dwell on the details, I do not skip them either.

If you are in the tender midst of your own healing, please take care of your nervous system. Read when you are ready. Pause when you need. Skip or return to parts as your spirit leads. There is no one right way to journey through a story like this. Your safety matters more than your completion.

This isn't a how-to or step-by-step self-help guide. This is my story. Written with trembling hands, cracked-open truth, and ink still wet from tears.

It's the kind of story that sits close to the skin. That asks nothing of you, except presence. These pages carry the weight of becoming. The mess and the magic. The breaking and the beauty.

They carry me.

Each word holds the frequency of vulnerability— a resonant strength that doesn't need applause to be authentic.

If you feel something while reading— a breath catch, a sting behind your eyes, a sudden remembering—know it's welcome here. This space was made with tenderness and truth.

Thank you for witnessing my story. Thank you for letting it breathe in your presence.

Your existence matters.
Your story ripples.
Your being here now—with me, with these words—means more than you know.

With love,
k. buehler

Introduction

"Sometimes, life is hard, sad, weird, and confusing. Sometimes, loss feels like a door closing on a room you never got to enter. But life, I've come to believe, is an invitation. We respond through living. Through experiencing. Through breathing our way into the unknown."
— k. buehler

This poignant quote encapsulates the essence of the poems and deeply personal narratives that k. buehler weaves into her masterfully crafted story —a profound exploration of grief, loss, trauma, and, ultimately, spiritual awakening and life wonderment. Life, as illustrated so vividly through her artfully written words, isn't a tidy straight line; it's a chaotic tapestry woven with threads of sorrow and struggle, yet also adorned with moments of unexpected beauty and grace.

I recall a mentor once sharing a powerful insight with me: in the face of adversity, we are presented with two paths. We can either rise up from our hardships, evolving into stronger, more grounded versions of ourselves—or we can allow those experiences to diminish us, leading to a shadow of our former selves.

Through this remarkable journey, she bravely invites us into her world—revealing a deep pursuit of presence and healing amidst heartrenching stories of trauma, grief, and loss. Her narrative highlights a powerful return to self, rooted in soul-level transformation and authentic truth.

Allow yourself to be enveloped by her profound honesty and the lyrical quality of her words and poetic vignettes. Embrace the opportunity to be fully present in her narratives—stepping into her soul as if you had experienced her journey firsthand. Perhaps, in doing so, you will uncover the valuable lessons she so gracefully imparts, guiding us all toward becoming more curious, more compassionate, and more awake in our own lives.

— Brad A. McCloskey

The Cocoon of Crisis

no one talks about
how the caterpillar
has to dissolve
not shift,
not simply grow wings
but melt
into something
unrecognizable
inside a dark, silent shell.

they say transformation
like it's a glow-up,
like it's poetry without
the blood.
but the truth?
it hurts.
it breaks you open
in places you thought
were already healed.

there's a moment
in the cocoon
when even hope
goes quiet.
when the old self weeps
for the life it lost
before the new self
has language
for the one it's becoming.

i've lived there.
in the middle.
in the ache.
in the grief of becoming.
scraping off stories
that no longer fit
and mourning the girl
who only knew how to
survive.

but here's the thing:
she loved me enough
to enter the dark.
to trust the undoing.
to believe, even trembling,
that maybe
this falling apart
was actually
a becoming.

and maybe
that's what it means
to transform—
to die a little
for the sake of flight.

the messy middle
by k. buehler

My biological dad was dying. I barely knew him. He had been in and out of prison most of my life. A shadow, more than a presence. Someone whose absence carved more shape into my story than his presence ever did.

And yet, in his final chapter, I found myself written in.

I became his Power of Attorney. I coordinated hospice. Navigated the legal system. Managed the medical decisions. I stood in that strange space between daughter and stranger, doing the work of love even though love had always felt... distant, complicated, fragmented.

In those final days—between hospital visits, prison calls, unanswered questions, and the kind of silence that hums louder than noise—I felt something begin to stir. There is a kind of clarity that only comes when you sit face-to-face with pain and refuse to look away.

I saw how much of my life I had spent proving—trying to earn love, approval, belonging. I saw how trauma had taught me to stay busy so I didn't have to feel. I saw how I had been preparing for something deeper, something I couldn't name yet—but could feel rising inside me.

And slowly, I began to remember.

I remembered that purpose isn't always shiny. It isn't always public. Sometimes, it's gritty and quiet and deeply personal. Sometimes it's the willingness to walk someone home—even if they never really walked beside you. Sometimes, it's choosing to stay open when everything in you wants to shut down.

In the quiet of that cocoon of crisis, I discovered something unexpected.

Words.

Not the kind I used in professional settings or strategy meetings. Different words. Truer. Softer. Heavier. I didn't know I was a poet until I stopped performing long enough to listen. Until the voice of k. buehler came through—not the achiever, but the feeler. Not the one with answers, but the one with questions and breath and ache.

The funny thing about transformation is that once you see your own unraveling as sacred—you start to see it everywhere. Even in your daughter.

I started writing this chapter the day my daughter's cat, Lulu, died.

She wrapped herself in a blanket like a cocoon and whispered through sobs, "Mama, can you just hold me? My heart feels like pieces that might not fit again."

And I did. I held her. Just like I had held myself in the hospice room, in the silence, in the letting go.

Yet Lulu's story doesn't start there. It started when Amelia was four and a half—with a pet rock.

Yes. A rock.

She named it Lulu. This rock went everywhere with her. Slept on her pillow. Traveled in pockets. Starred in photos. I stepped on it more times than I can count. Finally, in one of my not-best-mom moments, I told her, "If I step on that rock one more time, I'm throwing it away."

Of course, I stepped on it again. And I threw it away. She didn't just cry. She wept. For hours.

Weeks later, I looked out the window and saw her in the backyard playing with a cat. Pushing it on the swing. Guiding it up into her playhouse. Taking selfies with it on our phones. This went on for days.

Then our neighbor mentioned the cat was a stray and would be taken to the shelter. If the shelter didn't have space... it might not make it. Aaron and I looked at each other and that was that, "We'll take her."

Now, I have cat allergies. We had always said no to pets. But something about this moment—this particular cat—felt different. Destined.

I asked Amelia, "What do you want to name her?"

"Lulu," she said, no hesitation.

Then she looked up at me and added, "When you threw my Lulu rock away, God told me I would get a cat. And here she is."

So Lulu came home, and for the next few years she was love in feline form. Until the day she wasn't. Until the day my daughter wrapped herself in that blanket and asked to be held.

And again, I remembered.

Transformation always begins with a cracking. A falling apart. A loss. A goodbye. It never feels sacred when you're in it—but it is. This book isn't about avoiding pain. It's about honoring the process.

It's about how I found purpose in the ashes. How I discovered that the breaking point is often the becoming point. That the cocoon—the one that shows up in crisis, in hospice rooms, in heartbreak, in goodbye—is not a punishment. It's a passage.

This is the beginning—not of my pain, of the seed that planted my purpose and blossomed into my promise. And I'm inviting you in. Not to watch from the outside, but to sit beside me in the middle of the mess. Because maybe, just maybe, something here will meet you in your own cocoon.

Seven Souvenirs

Becoming begins in the breaking. The cocoon doesn't ask you to stretch—it asks you to dissolve. Transformation doesn't begin with flight. It begins with surrender.

You're not failing when it hurts. Pain is not proof you're doing it wrong. It's the pulse of something sacred unfolding. Grief is often the doorway to growth.

Crisis has a way of clarifying. When everything falls apart, what matters begins to rise. You begin to see what's true, what's yours, and what you no longer need to carry.

There is no timeline for your becoming. Healing doesn't wear a watch. Purpose doesn't work on deadlines. Give yourself the grace to go slow. To breathe. To just be.

Even the silence is speaking. The stillness. The questions. The quiet ache. These are not empty spaces —they are sacred chambers where something deeper is forming.

You'll grieve versions of yourself you once needed. Even if they were built from survival. Even if they helped you make it through. Letting them go is not betrayal—it's evolution.

You are held in the unraveling. Even when it feels like you're alone, you're not. Spirit. Love. Memory. Grace. They wrap around you like a cocoon, whispering: you are becoming.

Purposeful Ponderings

Where/When have you wrapped yourself in a metaphorical blanket and needed to be held?

What is trying to fall away in your life, and what might be trying to emerge?

Is there a voice inside you that you haven't made space to hear?

When was the last time you let yourself not be okay?

What if you stopped trying to "get over" the pain and started getting into the process?

What would it look like to trust the undoing?

Where in your life have you been both the stranger and the one who shows up?

What is your inner child still grieving that the world told you to forget?

Who or what are you being asked to hold—with no fixing, just presence?

Carried Then Cut Free

i was light
and the thing it burned
through.
a prayer
and the silence that
swallowed it.

i walked in with gold on
my tongue
and blood in my shoes.
they called it strength.
i called it
survival
with a better outfit.

some days i was rising.
some days i was
just not falling.
every day
i was both.

both
by k. buehler

One night before a board meeting, I got the text. I was sitting in the quiet, half-preparing for the next day's agenda, half-hoping for rest, when a message lit up my phone. It was from my biological father's wife. *"He has cancer. He wants you to call him."*

I hadn't seen him in nearly three decades. We'd only recently reconnected after I found him again as an adult. One meeting. Two hours. A few photos. A fragile thread between us—just enough to feel, not enough to make sense of what I was feeling.

And now he was dying.

I didn't know what to do with that. So I did what I had always done—I kept moving. I compartmentalized. I tucked the ache into a corner of my soul and wrapped myself in composure.

The next morning, I showed up like I always do—with a smile, a blazer, and the ability to speak power into rooms that still surprise me by opening their doors. I went to the meeting. I advocated for rural Iowa, for workforce equity, for youth opportunity. I shook hands. I gave updates. I celebrated momentum that had been years in the making.

No one in that room knew I had spent the night on the phone with a prison guard at a hospital. That I had been told my father had stage IV brain and lung cancer. That I would need to complete clearance forms to see him—because he was still incarcerated.

Somehow—God, Spirit, the universe, a call to Beth Townsend—made a way.

By that afternoon, I was standing at his bedside. He was thin. Shackled. Eyes full of a thousand things that didn't need to be said out loud. The doctor said he had weeks to live. Maybe days. And yet, somehow, there was peace in that room. He told me his only wish was to see me and my brothers again before he died.

We talked. I showed him pictures of Amelia and my brothers. He told me stories I didn't remember. Like how I won a peacemaker award in kindergarten. How I used to stop fights on the playground. How I stood between him and my younger brothers during his rages.

"I always knew you'd grow up to change lives," he told me.

That conversation didn't resolve everything. But it returned something. A piece of truth. A piece of me. And that was only the beginning.

What followed was a year that defied logic. A sacred paradox. A season where I held everything and nothing at once.

By day, I was leading nationally recognized efforts to transform public workforce systems. I was standing in rooms with congressional leaders and changemakers. Launching the Youth Systems Building Academy in D.C. Reimagining equity at local, state, and federal levels.

I won the Entrepreneur of the Year Tenacity and Grit Award from America's Small Business Development Center Iowa. Des Moines Business Record recognized me as a Forty Under 40.

I was writing and publishing articles about leadership and mentoring. I was speaking on national panels and helping reshape how rural communities think about opportunity.

From the outside, it looked like I was soaring. And I was. I was also unraveling.

Because behind the scenes, I wasn't just a leader.

I was a daughter navigating the legal system to get her father released from prison so he could die outside of a cell. I was an advocate managing ER calls, court hearings, hospice intakes, parole officers, and paperwork I didn't know I'd be asked to sign. I was answering calls from his wife—injured and confused and calling me ten times a day, forgetting each conversation. I was signing forms with trembling hands, trying to make decisions no daughter should ever have to make.

And at the very same time, I was still a mother. Still giving baths. Still grocery shopping. Still helping with homework and brushing out tangled hair and kissing scraped knees. Still folding laundry, cleaning up toys, and making birthday plans. Still trying to be emotionally, intimately, and sexually available for my partner—offering presence and connection when my own reserves were low.

There were nights I cried in hotel bathrooms after speaking on stage, wondering if I had anything left to give. There were mornings I made pancakes with a full heart and an empty soul.

I wasn't doing it alone. My support circle—my soul tribe—held me. They sent messages. They covered meetings. They sent flowers and food and prayers. They reminded me I didn't have to be everything to everyone every moment of every day. They helped me stay in all the places—physically and emotionally—when I wasn't sure I could.

There were moments I was holding it all together while quietly losing parts of myself I didn't know were still hurting. There were moments I stood on national stages in the afternoon and curled up in the dark with grief by night. There were moments I looked like a lighthouse and felt like the storm. There were moments I was both.

I had imagined my father dying peacefully at home. I had imagined a redemption arc. Instead, I watched him suffer. I watched him withdraw. I watched the system fail over and over again.

I also watched me. I watched myself rise. Not just in title or recognition—in truth.

I watched myself become someone I could be proud of. Not because I did it perfectly—because I did it fully. Because I let the pain pass through me, not become me.

Even as I grieved the father I never really had, I was becoming the daughter I needed to be—for myself.

Seven Souvenirs

Grief does not disqualify your leadership. In fact, it may be what softens you into the kind of leader the world needs—one who carries both truth and love. One with courage, confidence, and compassion.

Being seen doesn't always mean being understood. Recognition can applaud your strength, yet it rarely speaks to what it cost you.

Forgiveness is not erasure. It is choosing to set the pain down without pretending it never happened.

You don't need permission to mourn. Grief is holy even when it's messy. Especially when it's messy. Your sorrow does not need a story that makes sense to anyone else.

Your story is not a liability to your calling—it is the oil in the lamp. The flame burns brighter because of what you've walked through, not in spite of it.

There is room in you for more than one truth. You can be proud and aching. Brave and afraid. You can be the storm and the stillness. The wave and the anchor.

Healing is not something you earn by doing it well. It's not a performance. It's the slow, sacred unfolding of remembering that you are already whole, even as you become.

Purposeful Ponderings

What are you holding together that no one else can see?

What does it cost you to appear okay when you're unraveling inside?

Is there a voice inside you that you haven't made space to hear?

Where have you been both the lighthouse and the storm?

Are there parts of your story you've tucked away to keep functioning?

What is something you've been praised for that grew out of pain?

Who helped you stay in the room when you wanted to disappear?

What identities have you been juggling all at once?

What part of you is asking to be softened, even as you lead?

The Sacred Scattering

i unstitched it today— the threadbare memory
i'd kept folded like a grief-worn letter
tucked behind my ribs.

it was heavy once, a storm sewn into skin,
thunder in my throat every time someone said
forgive
like it was easy, like i hadn't already tried
a thousand ways to unbleed the ache.

but today i sat with the wound
not to fix it, to feel it—
to let it speak in its own tattered tongue.

and in its whisper, there was a softness.
not quite peace, but the beginning of
an ungripping.
so i exhaled the story— not to forget,
to stop reliving it as a punishment.

i gave the anger back to the wind.
let the shame sink into earth that knows
how to compost hurt.
i do not owe my suffering a shrine.
only a blessing as it goes.

and maybe that's what healing is:
a sacred scattering. a slow bloom
where once there was only survival.

unholding
by k. buehler

How do you grieve the loss of a father you hardly knew? How do you write his obituary? How do you thread the essence of a life when all you have are cold, hard facts and a handful of fractured memories? How are you supposed to feel? How do you heal?

There is no "right" answer to these questions.

Sometimes life is hard, sad, weird, and confusing. Sometimes loss feels like a door closing on a room you never got to enter. But life, I've come to believe, is an invitation. We respond through living. Through experiencing. Through breathing our way into the unknown.

Patrick Buehler's life—and his death—are part of my experience. His death offered me an invitation I didn't expect. An invitation to stop reliving the trauma like a ritual. An invitation to loosen the grip of shame I didn't even know I was still holding. An invitation to meet myself without judgment.

His search for peace ended in dying his death. My search for peace continues in learning to fully live my life. Because somewhere in the grief, I discovered something unexpected: Patrick Buehler—through the pain, the absence, the legacy—taught me how to see the light that can still come from darkness.

Pat Buehler Obituary

Patrick Ivar Buehler, 59, of Ottumwa, died at 10:07 p.m. October 5, 2023 at Keosauqua Health Center in Keosauqua.

He was born February 24, 1964 in Waterloo to Donald and Coyla Greenwood Buehler. He married Doris Rae Wilt on July 18, 1998.

Pat was a graduate of Cedar Rapids Washington High School. He worked as a machinist.

Pat was a loving husband and grandfather. He loved drawing, painting and anything artistic. He loved fishing and spending time on the river and in nature.

Surviving is his wife, Doris of Ottumwa; a daughter, Krista (Aaron) Tedrow of Ottumwa; granddaughter, Madyson Morgan of Ottumwa;

and a step-son, Adam Morgan of Ottumwa.

He was preceded in death by his parents; a brother, Daniel Merle Buehler; and two step-sons, Jason Morgan and Aaron Morgan.

His body has been cremated and no services are planned.

Reece Funeral Home is in charge of arrangements.

A few weeks before writing this obituary, my dear friend Teri asked if I had considered taking a solo trip somewhere warm to recuperate. She had taken many solo trips throughout her career and tenure wearing all the hats, daughter, sister, wife, mom, volunteer, leader, and the list goes on. She planted a seed, sent me a spreadsheet with some locations and dates then offered to help book it.

After a few weeks of thinking about it, I finally said yes to the trip.

I knew, somewhere deep in my body, it was time. I was running on fumes and faith. I needed rest, not the kind that sleep provides, the kind that restores your soul after it's been hollowed out by years of carrying things too heavy to name.

A few hours later, the phone rang.

He was gone.

I flew back from D.C., and in the two days that followed, I moved through the motions of death with the precision of someone who has had to become their own anchor too many times. I saw his body. Collected his ashes. Bought the urn. Wrote the obituary. Paid for the death certificate. Split ashes so his wife would have a part of him too.

And still, I kept showing up.

Yet something in me knew—I couldn't keep carrying all of this without a place to put it down.
So I took Amelia to Teri's. We sat in the hot tub under the sky, the contrast of warm water and night air softening my edges. I cried. I didn't know how to explain what I was feeling because there wasn't just one thing—there were layers. Grief.

Relief. Rage. Compassion. Exhaustion.

Underneath it all, I heard a quiet whisper, "Go." So we booked it.

And I boarded the plane with my father in my bag. His ashes, held in a temporary urn tucked inside my carry-on. Just him and me. On a trip he never took. On a trip I almost didn't let myself take.

What made it possible—what made it sacred—was not just my courage, it was my community. My Leadership Iowa cohort, who had become a second family, showed up with the kind of love that lingers. They sent messages, prayers, cards, texts, voicemails.

They didn't just stop there. They sent a gift—cash, so generous that it covered the financial burdens no one ever sees coming: the legal fees, the cremation, the paperwork... and the plane ticket. Because of their kindness, I was able to grieve without also drowning in financial stress. Because of their belief in me, I was able to go.

And then, suddenly, I was there.

In Mexico. Alone. Unplugged. Free. And terrified.

For the first time in my life, no one needed anything from me. No emails. No schedules. No urgent texts. No meetings. No stages. No spotlights. Just me, and the echoes of a life that had been lived entirely for everyone else.

I woke up that first morning in silence and cried— not out of sadness, it was a blend of exhaustion and confusion. Who was I without the noise? Without the service? Without the survival?

And then, I began to breathe. Deeply. Slowly. Like I was learning how for the first time.

I booked an excursion for the second day. That afternoon my dad and I boarded a boat with three other tourists and we set sail with our guides. It was the first and last time I went fishing with my dad.

When we got out on the deep sea I climbed to the front of the boat and held what I had left of the man who gave me my first last name. A man who wasn't ready to be a father to a daughter. A man who had been caged and thrown away.

I released him into the beautiful blue Caribbean— the place he had always dreamed of going but never did. Until I brought him, not in life, but in death. The water shimmered. The silence held me. I prayed. I wept. I forgave.

As the waves carried him, I felt them carry something from me too.

Later, as the other folks on the boat took turns reeling in a shark—nearly 200 pounds—we had to cut the line. The guide looked at me and said, "Your dad had a fighter spirit."

He did. So did I, and that's moment I realized I was ready to stop fighting.

Still, there was something unfinished. Something deeper that couldn't be healed through saltwater alone. That's when my friend Barb messaged me. She had sent me a link— to someone who could guide me through a healing experience. A shaman. In the jungle. Outside the city. The only time available was late at night.

Every part of me wanted to say no. Yet my soul whispered yes.

I waited until I was home to tell Aaron I'd been 20 miles from my hotel, in the middle of the night, in the jungle, with two shamans and a translator. I wasn't afraid of their intentions—I was afraid of the unknown. Of myself. Of what I might feel if I let go.

The healing lodge was small, enclosed, and pitch black. I have claustrophobia. I almost didn't go in. Then I remembered why I came.

So I entered the darkness. In an instant I was in the tiny cupboard I would push my brothers into when I started hearing voices get loud and glass shatter against the walls. I was six again, calming a toddler, cradling an infant, and wondering if it would be better to fall asleep forever.

Inside that sacred space, I let go of control. I let the prayers, the chants, the drumbeats move through me. I sat with the pain I had carried through decades and deaths. The grief of a little girl who never felt safe. The pressure of being the strong one. The shame of survival. The guilt of still being here.

There curled up on the hard stone, knees held to my chest, I sank into the darkness. I wept. I held myself and felt love wrapping around me. And something shifted. It wasn't loud. It wasn't theatrical.

It was ancient. Slow. Cellular.

I was not just releasing my father—I was releasing the parts of myself that only knew how to endure. I was unlearning the reflex to brace. I was letting love back in. When I walked out, I was different. Not fixed. Freer.

That's when I heard the whisper, "It's time to take off the cloak."

Seven Souvenirs

Grief doesn't always come from what was lost —sometimes it comes from what was never had. And naming that absence is an act of courage, not cruelty.

You don't need a perfect relationship to offer someone a beautiful goodbye. Closure isn't something you wait for—it's something you create with intention and love.

The body knows what the mind tries to ignore. If your spirit is aching for rest, it's not weakness. It's wisdom.

Healing may ask you to go somewhere unfamiliar— geographically, emotionally, spiritually. Go. The places that scare us often hold the pieces and peace we need.

Sometimes it takes distance to return to yourself. Being alone doesn't mean you're abandoned. It might mean you're finally coming home.

You can honor where someone came from without carrying their brokeness. You can say: this is yours, and this is mine—and still walk forward in peace.

The story doesn't end with the scattering. It begins with the bloom that only grows in the place you once thought was barren.

Purposeful Ponderings

What grief have you been holding that hasn't had language until now?

Have you ever felt guilty for needing rest, healing, or space to just be? Where does that guilt come from?

What does "release" mean for you—not just emotionally, but practically?

Is there a part of your identity you've been afraid to reclaim because of the pain associated with it?

When was the last time you were truly alone with yourself—no roles to fill, no one to serve? What did you notice?

Who or what helped you take your next step when you couldn't take it alone?

What have you been carrying out of obligation that you might now be ready to scatter with a blessing?

i don't know where
your pain started
but it traveled
through many people

until one day it found me

i saw your wound
then spoke the truth
you did to me
what was done to you

i don't know where
your pain started
but it stopped with me

cycles
by k. buehler

I began writing poetry during the last couple of days in Mexico—quietly at first, like someone sneaking sips from a sacred spring. The words came in whispers, then in waves. Something inside me had cracked open when I scattered my father's ashes, and from that fracture, a flood emerged.

I wrote without trying to make sense. I wrote like I was remembering a language I had forgotten I knew. I wrote because my body needed a way to speak what my mouth wasn't ready to say.

When I came home, the words followed me. And so did something else.

At first, it was just flashes—disturbing, confusing, almost surreal. Scenes I didn't recognize, but that felt viscerally familiar. Being recorded. In a room. With other children. Adults entering. The sense of being watched, directed. Violated.

I told myself it was a fluke. Maybe I had watched too many episodes of Law & Order: Special Victims Unit. Maybe my imagination was getting the better of me. Then... it happened.

A friend of mine, who was in the process of moving from California, gave me a call. He had recently bought a building in a neighboring town and was thinking about starting a youth center, so he invited me to tour an old YMCA. Part of the building had been updated and was functioning as a church. But the other half? It was deteriorating. Filthy. Forgotten.

We used flashlights to navigate the space. As we climbed the stairs, the realtor explained that this used to be the living quarters—where those who paid room and board would stay. That's when things started to feel... off.

We found rooms with padlocks on the outside. Scratch marks on the walls. Door handles removed. Deadbolts installed to keep people in, not out. Then my friend said something I'll never forget.

"Hey guys, check this out. My dad used to work on these in the early 90s. They were manufactured in California."

He was pointing to a large machine. It was a video

duplicator. An old one. Surrounding it were broken 8mm tapes.

Instantly, my body knew what my brain had been trying to deny. I hadn't been imagining things. I wasn't misremembering. I was in those rooms. I was in those videos. And I knew the man making those tapes... I had just released his ashes.

My stomach dropped. My breath vanished. I said nothing. We finished the tour. I stayed quiet. Numb.

As we were leaving, two people looked at me, concern in their voices, and asked, "Are you okay?"

I said I was fine. Then they pointed to my arms and my neck. Rashes. In the shape of handprints.

It was almost too much.

That night, I began to cry—for no apparent reason. The kind of crying that rises from somewhere ancient inside you. A weeping with no words.

Aaron asked what was wrong. I couldn't explain it. I told him I needed to go for a drive.

As I was walking out, Amelia stopped me.
"Mommy, you can tell me anything."
I love her heart.

I laughed gently, inside, at the impossibility of that invitation. How could I even begin to explain? I tried my best.

"When I was little," I told her, kneeling down, "some people did mean things to me. And I went to a place today where it happened. And it made me feel kinda sad. But I'll be okay."

I got in the car. And that's when it hit me—fully, clearly, irrevocably.

I am not only a survivor of child sexual abuse I am also a survivor of sex-trafficking and commercial childhood sexual abuse materials.

I had known for years that I'd been sexually violated by adults. I carried that awareness like a quiet bruise that never fully faded.

What I hadn't known—what I hadn't let myself remember—was the unthinkable.

That as a child, I had been sold. People paid to abuse me. I was coerced into abusing other children. And people paid to watch it.

The memory crashed over me like a tidal wave. I didn't know what to do with it. It felt too big. Too awful. Too far outside the narrative I had carefully constructed to make sense of my pain. I had always placed myself in the role of the one harmed —and I was.

I now saw I had also been used to harm others. Not by choice. Not with understanding. Not with consent.

Through manipulation. Through grooming. Through the warped machinery of abuse that turns innocence into a weapon against itself.

And it broke me open.

I knew about sexual exploitation of children. I had attended and facilitated training on the topic in my advocacy work. How was I just now realizing this?

How do you even begin to hold that kind of truth? How do you grieve what was done to you and what was done through you—when you were still a child? How do you forgive the parts of yourself that didn't know better—because no one ever protected you enough to know there was a better?

I didn't have answers. Only waves of nausea. Of rage. Of unbearable sorrow.

My drive led me to the front of an old country church. I found myself sitting beneath a tree planted in memory of my grandmother. It is a place I often go when I need clarity, or comfort, or courage.

As I sat there, I heard a whisper—not out loud, in that sacred place where intuition speaks.

"It's time to take off the cloak. I need you to thank me for what happened."

I recoiled. What? Thank you? For that?

The whisper came again. "Thank me for the experience."

I shook my head. No. Absolutely not.

A third time: "Do you trust me? If you do, I need you to thank me for that experience."

I didn't want to. But I did trust.

So with tears in my eyes and fire in my throat, I whispered: "I don't want to thank you. I don't really mean it. But I trust you... so fine... thanks for the experience."

And in that moment, something extraordinary happened.

I saw a vision, like a fast-flipping comic book. Every moment of harm I had endured, every abuser, every scene. Then, alongside each person, another story began to unfold. Their pain. Their history. Their own origin wounds.

It stretched back generations. Hundreds of books. A lineage of hurt passed down like inheritance.

And then—all the books started closing. Until only one remained. Mine.

And when mine closed, I heard: "You needed to thank me because it stops with you."

I was stunned. Silenced. Awakened.

Then came the final whisper: "Do you think you'd be able to do the work you do with youth, to impact and change systems, and to have the influence you have without those experiences?"

I knew the answer. That was the moment I understood: I had chosen this life. This story. This body. This purpose.

I forgave myself for choosing the pain.
I thanked myself for surviving.
And I blessed myself for becoming.

When I got home, I wrote. As I poured words onto the pages I discovered more about the girl and woman I was learning to love. She really was something incredible.

Seven Souvenirs

You don't have to explain your silence.
Sometimes we stay quiet to survive. Reclaiming your voice doesn't require an apology.

You can be both the keeper of hard memories and the author of a new story. The past may shape us, but it doesn't get to define us.

Memory doesn't always arrive gently.
Sometimes it comes through cracked doors and rashes and flash-backs. That doesn't make it less true. It makes it holy

The truth may feel too heavy to hold at first.
Hold it with compassion and it will stop holding you hostage.

There is a difference between remembering and reliving. When you remember with love, you begin to rewrite what was written without your permission.

The body carries what the mind forgets (or buried to protect you). Listening to your body can reveal truths that language hasn't yet reached.

The pain may not have started with you—but it can stop with you. Not through erasure - through presence, truth, and transmutation.

Purposeful Ponderings

What part of your story have you been too afraid to fully look at?

What parts of your story have you kept quiet—out of fear, habit, or protection?

Are there memories you've doubted or dismissed because they seemed too painful—or too impossible—to be true?

How does your body communicate what words sometimes can't?

When was the last time you were truly alone with yourself—no roles to fill, no one to serve? What did you notice?

What do you need to forgive your younger self for believing about you?

What truth does that younger you need to hear now?

Who or what has helped you hold the weight of what surfaced?

What part of your voice is ready to be un-muffled?

What truth are you ready to write—not because it's easy, because it's yours?

The Reclamation

i learned early:
quiet girls get gold stars
& wild hearts get detention.
so i pressed my poems
into the folds of my skin,
hid the crescendos
in my spine
& bit back the bloom of words
before they could dare
become song.

they called it "good behavior"
but it felt like burial.
every no i couldn't say
grew a thorn in my throat.
every truth swallowed
made a graveyard of my gut.

i dressed my fire in soft syllables.
practiced platitude
like it was a virtue.
ironed out my voice
until it fit in the silence
they handed me.

but inside—
inside, i was opera.
symphony.
drumbeat & howl.
a language
that refused extinction.

now—
i am the girl who spills
what they told me
to swallow.
the woman who writes
what they said
no one would read.

muffled
by k. buehler

I didn't know that publishing a book would feel like holding a part of my soul in my hands. The first time I touched the draft edition of my poetry, I felt it throughout my entire being. Not because it was perfect. Not because I had finally "arrived." Because something I had buried for decades had finally emerged from the silence.

It began with a whisper in Mexico. A line here, a phrase there. Then, like a storm finally finding its sky, the poems poured out of me. What I once thought were scattered feelings and fragmented memories began weaving themselves into verse. Writing became a way to hold what I couldn't carry in conversation.

After the remembering came the reclaiming.

I didn't set out to become a poet/author. I became one because it was the only language my soul could speak after everything I had held inside finally broke open. When I got home, I kept writing. In the early morning, before the world stirred. In the quiet moments after putting Amelia to bed. On grocery lists, in the margins of notebooks, on my phone in parking lots.

The words kept coming. They weren't always polished. Yet they were mine. And for the first time in my life, that was enough.

I heard that whisper again. The same one I heard under the tree planted in memory of my grandmother, just days after the deepest remembering of my life.

I heard the whisper clearly: "Publish it."

At some point, I made a promise to myself. Not for the world—for me. It felt like a vow. And I meant it.

Months passed. Life kept moving. I poured myself into the work I was known for—writing grants, developing programs, advocating for others. Then one day, while I was knee-deep in crafting two more grant proposals—for two different organizations—I caught a glimpse of myself in the reflection of my laptop screen. And it hit me. There I was making dreams possible for others while putting mine on hold.

I had promised to publish. And I still hadn't. I

would have moved heaven and earth to keep a promise to someone else... So why was I still breaking promises to me?

It was a painful realization.

No wonder I didn't fully trust myself. No wonder something still felt incomplete.

So I stopped everything and made a new kind of commitment: I wasn't going to wait for the perfect time. I wasn't going to wait for permission. I wasn't going to wait to be chosen.

I was going to publish the damn book. (Shout out to my friend Hollie Tometich, Author of *Buy The Damn Shoes,* available on Amazon.)

I did not just want to publish it any way it could be done — I wanted to own my voice completely.

Self-publishing on Amazon KDP is straight-forward if you go the easy route. They offer a free International Standard Book Number (ISBN), but here's the truth: when they own the ISBN, they technically own the distribution rights to your work. And this—this wasn't just a creative project.

It was my healing. My voice. My name. My story.

So I launched my own publishing imprint. Bought my own ISBNs. And let me tell you, it's no small thing:
- One ISBN costs $125.
- Ten ISBNs? $1,000. No in-between. No equity for emerging authors—just a steep price for sovereignty.
- Each format—paperback, hardcover, eBook, audiobook, even a downloadable PDF—requires its own ISBN.
- If you want to copyright it officially, you spend another $150, fill out a mountain of paperwork, and send two copies to the Library of Congress.

It's not glamorous. It's tedious. It was sacred. And I was willing to do the work—because I was finally keeping a promise to myself.

Then came a moment I hadn't prepared for. Aaron read the proof copy. A few days later, he got quiet.

Then he gently and honestly told me he was upset. He felt like he should've heard some of those stories from me directly—that it hurt to read about them instead of having been invited into them.

And I understood. I really did. He wasn't trying to control the story. He was trying to be part of the healing. Yet something rose up in me—something steady, strong, and deeply true.

I told him, as hot tears spilled down my cheeks, "Some of the things I wrote... I hadn't even talked about with myself yet. Writing them was me finally facing them. This isn't about leaving you out. This is about letting myself in."

Then I looked him in the eyes and said, "This is my story. I get to share it when, where, and how I choose."

He paused. Listened. Softened. Then he apologized.

I thanked him, because I knew it came from love—from wanting to protect, not to possess.

I told him that what had actually helped heal me most... were the moments I did share things with him—and he didn't flinch.

He never looked at me differently. Never loved me less. If anything, he loved me more completely. That gave me the courage to keep writing.

I invited him to read the second poetry collection before it was published. He's more of an audiobook guy, so I'm not sure he finished it—and I'll invite him to read this one too.

Because this is our story now. Not just the publishing. The becoming.

The becoming of someone who trusts her own voice. Someone who keeps her promises. Someone who doesn't wait to be chosen—because she already is.

Seven Souvenirs

A promise to yourself is sacred. It might not scream for your attention like other commitments do—yet when you keep it, something inside you begins to heal.

You don't need to be chosen to be worthy. Sometimes the most important recognition is your own.

Reclamation rarely looks like arrival. It looks like quiet courage. Like sending the email. Buying the ISBN. Printing the page. Naming the thing.

You are allowed to hold space for others and still show up for yourself. Supporting everyone else doesn't mean you abandon your own voice.

Your story is yours. You get to share it when, where, and how you choose. No one else gets to decide when you're "ready."

Love can coexist with discomfort. Sometimes the people who love us most will need time to understand how we heal. That doesn't make your healing any less valid.

Trusting yourself isn't a one-time moment. It's a slow rebuilding. Each time you choose your truth, your voice, your art—you're coming home.

Purposeful Ponderings

What promises have you made to yourself—and quietly broken?

Is there something creative or sacred you've been postponing for the sake of others?

How do you know when you're honoring your voice?

Are there parts of your story you're afraid to share, not because they're untrue, but because they're still tender?

What does it mean to belong to yourself first?

Have you ever felt unseen or misunderstood when you started speaking your truth? How did you respond? How would you like to?

If you gave yourself full permission to take up space—to publish, to speak, to rise—what would you do next?

The Space Between Us

i didn't grow in spite of you
i grew with you.
beside your quiet fears
and your steady hands.
in the pause between your doubts
and the way you still showed up.

you never held me back.
you held me,
even when i reached
toward the sky.

i know you feel
like a shadow
to the brightness in me—
but you should know,
my light found its shape
in your reflection.

this isn't about who's ahead
or who's behind.
this is about
two people
with sore hearts
trying to find
a shared horizon
through the fog.

maybe the road bends now.
maybe it doesn't.
please don't call yourself
a hindrance
to the healing
you helped me find.

you've mattered.
you still do.
and no matter
where our paths lead—
you are not
less worthy
of the love
we created together.

two people, one horizon
by k. buehler

Healing within a relationship is rarely straight-forward. It's a sacred, complicated dance— especially when two people are still learning how to hold their own pain without handing it to each other. Aaron and I didn't arrive here easily. We're still arriving. Still unfolding.

The year my father was dying— the year I was flying back and forth from conferences, juggling national projects, coordinating his release from prison, driving his wife to visit him behind bars, managing hospice and end-of-life care, that year stretched me in every possible way.

I was leading big systems-change work, while quietly unraveling. I had done counseling and emotional healing work. I had coping tools.

I didn't have the capacity for everything that surfaced all at once— the suppressed memories, the body flashbacks and flareups, the financial pressure of funeral expenses and legal fees, the reality of holding space for so many people and not having much space left for myself.

And of course it strained my relationship with

Aaron. How could it not? He was often solo-parenting while I was gone. And if I'm honest—often even when I was home. I was physically present but emotionally tapped out. Raw. Hyper-vigilant. Especially when it came to how he interacted with Amelia.

Looking back, I see it more clearly. The tension. The exhaustion. The ways we were both overwhelmed and under-supported. The way we loved each other, but kept missing each other.

There were moments I had to sit with a kind of truth I never expected to name—not just about him, about me. About what I was willing to tolerate. What I was unknowingly recreating. And what I had to finally break in order to begin again.

There were no bruises. But that didn't mean there wasn't harm. Sometimes it was his tone. Sometimes it was the slammed door. Sometimes it was a hole in the wall. The way objects flew across the room. The way Amelia's shoulders curled in just slightly—enough for me to notice. Enough for me to feel the ache of my own childhood pulse through hers.

Sometimes—it was me. My tone. My impatience. The way I snapped when I was depleted. The way I shut down, or rushed past what needed presence. I had been the "strong one" for so long. But strength doesn't always mean softness. And I had to face the ways my own unhealed pain shaped how I showed up, too.

Just because someone isn't hitting you doesn't mean they aren't breaking something. Just because someone loves you doesn't mean they're safe—until they choose to be. And just because you've survived doesn't mean you've stopped the cycle.

That takes intention. And boundaries. And truth-telling.

I had promised myself that my daughter would not grow up apologizing for being a child. That she wouldn't inherit my silence. Or someone else's rage. That she wouldn't be conditioned to tiptoe around another person's unregulated emotions, including mine. So I spoke the truth out loud.

I told him: I love you. I believe in your healing.

Because of that, I will not allow our child—or myself—to carry wounds that do not belong to us. The yelling. The intimidation. The throwing. The slammed doors. It ends now.

It wasn't a threat. It was a boundary. One that honored us both. He pushed back at first. Told me not to threaten him. I stayed steady.

"This is the truth," I said. "I will honor it—even if you don't."

Something shifted. Not instantly. But eventually. I watched the shame wash over him. Watched him spiral into self-blame.

I told him: "I love you too much to let you keep hurting yourself by hurting us."

Love, I'm learning, isn't just softness. It's structure. It's accountability. It's seeing the divine in someone, and refusing to let them remain a stranger to it.

In the middle of all that—grief, confrontation, exhaustion—something unexpected happened. I began the long, slow work of learning to like my body.

This body that had been taken, praised, used, ignored. Given for birth. Offered for pleasure. Pressured into performance. Rarely, if ever, fully mine. I realized that healing my voice was not enough. I had to heal the vessel that carried it.

I began to notice how I flinched when Aaron reached for me— not because I didn't love him, because my body still didn't feel like it belonged to me. It wasn't that I didn't want connection. I just wanted choice. I wanted to initiate, not brace. To be touched with presence, not assumption.

We talked—really talked. About how his love sometimes looked like entitlement. About how my survival looked like silence. Then on a blue moon night, under a heavy sky, he said something that unstitched us both.

"I don't think we've ever really made love. We've had sex. We've loved each other. But we've never loved ourselves enough to meet each other fully in that space."

He apologized. For taking it personally when I said no. For pushing past my body's boundaries in subtle yet violating ways. For assuming access instead of seeking consent.

I felt a weight lift off of me. Because he finally saw it. And because I finally felt it.

My body is not a debt to be paid. It's not a prize to be earned. It's not a container for someone else's desire. It is mine.

I'm learning to love my body—not because it's perfect, because it is worthy of being safe, held, and whole.

Aaron and I are still in it. Still figuring it out. We know that maybe it's forever and maybe it's not. We get to choose. Now, there's breath in the space between us. There's more softness. There's more safety. There's mutual becoming.

And that is its own kind of love story.

Seven Souvenirs

You can love someone deeply and still need boundaries. Love and limits are not opposites. In fact, true love often requires them.

Emotional safety is just as vital as physical safety. Words, tones, reactions, and silences leave marks too. Pay attention to how the air feels between you.

Your body is not a tool for someone else's healing. You are not responsible for how others process your truth. You are responsible for honoring your own.

Silence is not the same as peace. Just because it's quiet doesn't mean it's healthy. Sometimes silence is just survival in disguise.

Healing isn't always loud—it's often in the choosing. Choosing to stay present. Choosing to say "not this." Choosing to come home to your body. Choosing yourself.

You don't have to fix someone to love them. You do have to protect yourself and your children from their unhealed wounds.

It's okay to grow differently. Healing may not look symmetrical. One of you may remember first. One of you may say sorry first. That doesn't mean you're not growing together—it means you're human.

Purposeful Ponderings

Where do I feel safest in my relationship—and where do I feel like I shrink?

Have I been honest with myself about what my body needs? How do I know when I'm ignoring those needs?

Are there moments I've excused harmful behavior because I understand where it came from?

What boundaries have I set with others—but still struggle to hold with myself?

How do I define love that is both tender and accountable?

What does it mean for me to truly like my body—not just love it in theory?

What might change if I believed I didn't have to earn safety, affection, or rest?

Finding Me

i walked into the forest
to escape,
and found myself instead.

each tree stood as a reminder:
there is no rush to grow.
there is no shame in standing
still.
there is no weakness in
reaching
for the light.

love is like the forest—
dense, layered,
a place where shadows and
light
coexist.

it's here, in this tangle,
that i learn who i am.

the forest within
by k. buehler

After reclaiming my body and learning to speak my truth inside relationship, there came a quieter, deeper invitation— one that didn't shout or shake me awake. One that sat beside me and was curious and compassionate, inviting me to conversation.

Can you trust yourself now? Not just in crisis. Not just in resilience. In the sacred ordinary of being alive. Not in performance. Not in perfection. Not in codependence masked as connection.

In the kind of trust that grows slowly—like a plant learning the shape of its own roots. The kind that says: "I choose me, even when no one else does."

Self-trust, it turns out, isn't a destination. It's a practice. A muscle. A rhythm. And for me, it began to strengthen in the quietest of ways.

A year after scattering my father's ashes into the Caribbean, a year after my body remembered what it had survived, a year after beginning to write again— I took a three-day retreat. Just me.

No child. No partner. No agenda. Three days. Alone. A quiet cabin in the woods. A few hikes.

Some journaling. A movie by myself. No schedule. No one needing me. Just me.

And I'll be honest—it felt radical. Almost wrong.

I'm a mom. A wife. A caregiver. A consultant. A space-holder. I'm used to showing up, checking in, holding it all together. For those three days—I didn't.

And it wasn't easy. That little voice whispered constantly: Shouldn't you be home? Shouldn't you be folding laundry or answering emails? This is indulgent. Selfish. Lazy.

Nevertheless, I persisted. I kept showing up to the quiet anyway. I hiked without rushing. I wrote—without a deadline, without a filter. I sat still long enough to hear myself again.

Slowly, I reconnected to the version of me who didn't need to perform or prove or please. That's when the poems came—fast and unfiltered. I wrote more than half the pieces that would become *Finding Me* in that cabin. They poured out of me like a flood long held back by survival.

Each word a breadcrumb back to myself.

That time alone didn't mean I was abandoning my family. It didn't mean I didn't love my daughter or my partner or the work I'm called to do. It just meant I was finally loving myself, too.

I began asking: What do I actually want? before asking: What do they need from me?

I discovered moments that became reclamations. The slow mornings without urgency. The playlists that made my lungs remember joy. The long walks where I prayed without words. The candles lit to take a moment to reflect and connect with my creator. The clothes that felt like my soul, not just my role.

Creatively— I stopped asking if I was too much. I stopped seeking permission. I wrote what I once would've buried. And I let that be enough.

Spiritually— I returned to the still voice. Sometimes prayer looked like tears. Sometimes like trees. Sometimes like a deep breath when I didn't have words.

Sexually— I felt the bracing slow down. I let no be a full sentence. I let yes mean something again. I chose touch. I chose stillness. I chose me.

Emotionally— I let myself unravel without rushing the reassembly. With each choice—each boundary, each breath, each poem— I came back to myself.

There were moments I noticed the shift: When I walked into a room and didn't shrink. When I rested without guilt. When I made a decision without explaining it. When I looked in the mirror and whispered, "I'm proud of you," and meant it.

This return—this becoming— isn't a destination. It's a daily devotion. A practice. A promise kept to myself. And every time I choose me, I remember: I am not waiting to be found. I was here all along.

The truth I keep returning to: Finding yourself isn't always a clear path. It's not a checklist. It's not a one-time epiphany. It's messy, murky, ever-evolving.

And sometimes, even when you think you have

arrived, something knocks on your chest and reminds you— you've still got more to uncover.

There are days I feel rooted in myself. Clear, grounded, alive. And there are days I notice, only after the fact, that I gave too much of me to something that didn't feel aligned. That I swallowed my truth to keep the peace. That I shrank a little. That I said yes when my body meant no.

In those moments, the old voice tries to creep in: You should've known better. You're supposed to be further along than this. You're supposed to be the healed one now.

I honor that voice. It reminds me of how I used to think. It is a voice that I know is trying to protect me that doesn't realize the harmful tone. I thank it and remind it of what I know: There's no "right" way to find yourself. There's only the way that honors your becoming. And that it looks different for each of us.

For me, it looked like a cabin in the woods and writing poetry on the floor. For Aaron, it looked like taking a week off from work and riding his motorcycle solo to Montana. Long roads. Open sky. Wind on his back. Space to sort through the noise. A different kind of solitude. A different kind of remembering.

We each find ourselves in our own way. And there is no shame in that. There is no expiration date on discovery. There is no failure in forgetting. Only another chance to come home to yourself again.

So if you're still in the fog... If you've lost your voice again... If you handed your power to something or someone who didn't know how to hold it with care— It's okay.

You're not broken. You're not late. You're not wrong. You're just human. Becoming. Still and always becoming.

The invitation remains: Return. Whenever you're ready. You don't need to explain. You can just show up.

Seven Souvenirs

Self-trust grows in silence. It often isn't loud or immediate. It speaks in quiet nudges, body-sensations, gut-checks, and that moment you realize, "I knew this all along."

You won't always get it right—and that's okay. Sometimes you'll override your inner knowing. Sometimes you'll realize after the fact. The win is in noticing. The healing is in returning.

It's not about never needing others. It's about knowing when you're asking from a place of connection rather than seeking validation or outsourcing your worth.

Self-trust looks like boundaries. The ones you hold with others, yes—especially the ones you hold with yourself. The "I won't abandon me again" kind.

Your daily moments matter. Whether it's a slow cup of tea, a playlist that unlocks joy, a walk at sunset, or a poem you whisper to your own reflection—your practices are your prayers.

You can't rush embodiment. Knowing and doing are different. Be patient with the space between awareness and action. That space is where transformation happens.

Self-trust is remembering, again and again, that you are safe with you. That your voice matters. That your pace is enough. That your life gets to feel like your own.

Purposeful Ponderings

What moments in your life taught you to distrust yourself? Whose voices do you still carry that make you second-guess your knowing?

What practices/habits/rituals make you feel most like you? What simple practices could you reclaim to create small moments of sovereignty?

When was the last time you made a choice purely because it felt aligned with your truth, not out of obligation, fear, or expectation?

How do you respond to yourself when you "get it wrong"?

What would it look like to offer yourself the same grace you offer others?

Where do you still wait for permission? What decision—small or large—have you been postponing until someone else says, "Yes, it's okay"?

What would your life look like if you fully trusted your voice, your body, your spirit, and your story?

What does coming home to yourself mean today—not someday, but now?

The Cloak

they told me god lived
in buildings and books,
with guilt-stitched sermons
about sin-shaped shadows.

yet when i lit a candle
in solitude and silence,
god came softly.
not as judge,
as warmth.
not as fear,
as frequency.

i stopped kneeling to shame
and started listening
to starlight.

and there,
in the hush of my own
becoming,
i heard god say:
"finally. you've found me
where i've always been—
inside you."

unlearning god
by k. buehler

I didn't set out to reinvent my entire belief system. I just wanted to feel free. Free from the guilt. Free from the shame. Free from the invisible weight of trying to earn love, approval, or "holiness."

After decades of performing faith, carrying trauma, and mistaking fear for reverence, I felt a quiet call in my spirit—an invitation to take off the cloak. Not just the one I wore for others, the one I had unknowingly wrapped around my own soul.

The cloak of silence. The cloak of obedience. The cloak of "should."

Underneath it, I began to find myself. I started getting curious—not just about who I was, about what I believed. Not what I had been told to believe. Not what was passed down through doctrine or trauma or tradition. What I actually believed.

I began to explore things I had been taught were "evil." Astrology. Tarot. Sound healing. Sacred movement like somatic yoga.

I soon realized—ignorance really does foster fear

and hate. When I slowed down long enough to listen, I could feel the resonance. I didn't feel fear. I felt wonder.

I discovered that one of the reasons tarot cards were created was to help communicate stories from the Bible to poor and working class people who couldn't read. Each image was a visual cue—accessible, portable, and sacred—like the parables Jesus told. A tool for equity, not idolatry.

They were never meant to be feared. They were meant to bring light to the people. To help them see truth for themselves without needing to pay a priest or enter a building to access God. Just like Jesus did.

And the stars—the ones I had been told to avoid—they spoke, too. I figured if the wise men were led by stars to find Jesus, then maybe there was wisdom there. Maybe the heavens do declare the glory of God.

Maybe the night I was born carries clues about the blueprint I carry. After all, as the great scientist Carl Sagan said, "We are made of star stuff."

My curiosity didn't lead me away from God. It led me deeper into the presence of heaven. It led me home.

During this time, I also transitioned into a new season professionally. After years of working multiple jobs, consulting, and being the youngest Workforce Board Executive Director in the country, I shifted into a role with more flexibility and less responsibility. I stepped back from managing and volunteering for everything—and leaned into creating. To detoxing from over-working. To remembering who I was without the pressure of being "on" all the time.

I also became certified as a sound healer and astrologer. I studied ancient healing modalities like acupuncture and the medicine of energy and music. I began to merge the sacred and the scientific.

One of the most healing conversations I had with God started like this: "If all my kids live in different places, look different, have different cultures and languages, why wouldn't they all have different names for me?"

The veil of religion began to thin. I wasn't sure what that meant for me yet and I also knew I couldn't unsee what I had seen. I couldn't unknow what I had come to know.

In that tender, liminal space—somewhere between unraveling and becoming—several women held space for me. Sacred space. Unspoken, unconditional space. They didn't try to fix me or preach at me. They didn't offer answers. They offered presence. And that was everything.

I don't have all of them listed here. However, I need to honor a few.

Rachelle is a two-time college president at faith-based institutions—the first female president at both. She's brilliant. Bold. Grounded in her own faith. Over the course of my career, Rachelle poured into me as a mentor and leader. And in this season, she poured into me as a woman. As a seeker. She was intentional about calling and checking in, even when I didn't call or text back. She never rushed me, never judged. Her presence was a balm. A reminder that you don't have to have it all together to be deeply loved.

Lauren has seen me at my worst. One of the first times we met she literally pulled glass out of my backside. She's always been there to help me process the hard stuff and has been an anchor. She invited me into her family and I became an honorary member of the Smiths. She showed me what healthy families look like and has loved me and celebrated me through all the highs and the lows, every moment.

Nicole has been one of my best friends for over a decade. The kind of friend who doesn't wait for the perfect moment—she just shows up. She picked up Amelia, helped clean my house, dropped everything to drive me to the hospital the day after I got the text that changed everything. She has cried with me, laughed with me, carried burdens with me. Her love is quiet and fierce—the kind of steady that holds space even when I couldn't speak.

Barb and Hollie are both leaders, advocates, and dreamers. Women who understand what it means to build something from scratch while holding space for others. They are justice-driven, equity-focused, deeply rooted in purpose—and they've championed me in my career, in my community work, and in my becoming. They reminded me that you can be soft and strong, visionary and vulnerable.

Calan and Liesl are part of my Leadership Iowa family—sisters born of deep conversations, shared meals, and truth-telling walks. Calan booked a girls' weekend when I didn't even know how much I needed one. We got massages, rested, and just breathed. She didn't ask for anything—she just made space.

Liesl is like a big sister. A powerful rural advocate, a steady friend. She traveled with me on work trips, walked alongside me (literally and figuratively), and held space for my questions without trying to offer answers. When I was struggling silently, she spoke up to our Leadership Iowa family on my behalf—and their response was generous, heartfelt, and healing.

Yvonne—my hairdresser turned heart-friend—met me in a season of slow unraveling and quiet becoming. I lovingly call her my hairapist because our appointments were never just about hair.

They were soul sessions. Conversations braided with faith, poetry, neurodivergence, motherhood, and the sacred mess of running a small business.

We didn't always agree, but agreement was never the point. There was no judgment—only presence. Even after I stopped attending the church where we met, it was never weird, never tense—just real, rooted friendship. The kind that doesn't need matching theology to hold unconditional space.

Teri and Ashley—my leaders, my mentors, my anchors in a season of unraveling and rebuilding. When I transitioned out of the most high-profile role of my career, it was Teri—my board vice chair at the time—who applied for the role and took the torch. It was Teri and Ashley who created a safe space for me to land. A place where I could detox from overwork, show up as I was, and breathe again.

They carried so much wisdom about motherhood, leadership, womanhood—and they held me with gentleness and grace as I remembered who I was beyond performance. They didn't just manage me —they cared for me. And I will never forget that.

Never once—never once—did any of these women judge me for asking hard questions. They didn't flinch when I wondered aloud about scripture, spiritual trauma, or the dogma I was disentangling from. They didn't try to fix me or correct me. They listened. They stayed. They let me unravel, and then helped me remember I could also re-weave.

These women saw me not as broken— as becoming. Not just as colleagues or co-conspirators— as sisters on the journey. The space they held for me—I'll never fully find the words to explain what it meant. I'll never forget it. Because when I was afraid that asking questions would cost me love, they gave me more.

Slowly, gently, I began to believe that maybe my light wasn't a threat. Maybe it was a gift. Maybe the parts of me that didn't fit in religious boxes weren't rebellious—they were radiant. Maybe heaven had been within me all along.

Yet there was still one pillar standing. While many of the old beliefs had been dismantled, while I had found new language and new freedom, there was still a question I hadn't let myself fully hear.

That—gentle, knowing—whisper asked it again: "Do you think you need church to be good with Me?"

I paused.

"No," I said. "I don't think so. Do I?"

God responded, "Don't go. Let's see if you believe it."

I wanted to believe it. I thought I believed it. I also kept going. Week after week, I sat in the pews. I sang the songs. I took notes. Then something began to shift.

The messages—once comforting—began to hurt. The so-called "good news" felt wrapped in shame, sin, and scarcity. So many sermons fixated on death, wrath, and unworthiness.

I found myself hearing harm from the people I once stood beside. I didn't like how they weaponized scripture. How they spoke about love while preaching fear. How they offered salvation by shaming people into it. Still—I couldn't stop going.

Because the truth was: I did think I needed church to be okay with God. I did believe that not going would mean I was out of alignment, off track, unworthy.

This was the last pillar to shake. And when it finally did, it rattled me to my core. I have always identified with faith. I have always known, deep down, that I wasn't alone.

I saw angels when I was a child—real ones. Wings wrapped around me and my brothers as we crouched behind furniture and in cupboards while my birth parents screamed, sharp objects flying, my mother bleeding.

I remember running barefoot to the neighbor's house, my heart pounding, begging them to call for help because I thought my mom might not survive. The angels were with me. They spoke to me. They told me how to keep my brothers safe. I never doubted they were real.

Then... I was adopted. The family that brought me in went to church. Eventually, they became pastors. On Sundays, they preached love and righteousness. Yet the rest of the week... wasn't always loving or righteous.

Still, church gave me something I desperately craved— a sense of belonging. A "faith family." A place to be chosen. A place to be good.

So even as I deconstructed everything else— even as I rewrote my understanding of sin, grace, and God— I clung to that last piece. Because church had been my identity. My security. My home.

Letting it go felt like losing another family. And yet... the Voice in me stayed steady.

"I never lived in that building," God whispered. "I've always lived in you. Are you ready to take off the cloak?"

I was. It was time. As I slowly slipped it off, my light began to really shine.

Seven Souvenirs

You don't have to reject everything to reclaim yourself. Deconstruction isn't about destruction—it's about discernment. You can honor what shaped you and still outgrow it.

Curiosity is sacred. The questions you're afraid to ask are often the doorway to deeper connection. Wonder is not rebellion—it's revelation.

Spirituality is not a performance. God never asked you to audition for love. Holiness isn't something you prove. It's something you remember.

Tradition is not the same as truth. Just because something has been taught for generations doesn't mean it's aligned with love. Test every teaching by its fruit: Does it free or does it bind?

Your body remembers what your spirit already knows. If a space, sermon, or system causes shame or fear, your resistance might be wisdom—not disobedience.

Leaving doesn't mean losing. You can walk away from harmful beliefs and still walk with God. You don't stop being spiritual when you stop being performative.

Taking off the cloak is not betrayal—it's becoming. It's not about turning your back on faith. It's about turning your face toward the light that's always lived within you.

Purposeful Ponderings

What beliefs have you held that were rooted more in fear than freedom? Where did they come from—and are they still serving you?

What would it feel like to explore your spirituality without guilt or pressure? To simply be with God/the Divine in the quiet, without performance?

When have you felt most connected to God/ Source/ Spirit? What were you doing—or not doing?

Who has held space for you during your spiritual evolution? Who helped you feel safe to ask the hard questions? How can you honor them—or become that for someone else?

What are the "cloaks" you've worn—beliefs, roles, performances—that it might be time to set down?

What practices, tools, or traditions once labeled as "evil" or "off-limits" are actually sources of healing or wisdom for you now?

If God really lives in you—how would your life, your faith, your love look different?

Curious You PhD In Me

you are an echo of what has
been forgotten—
the wisdom of wonder,
the freedom of love,
the audacity of dreaming.

how do we remember
what it means to know
ourselves?
not the self they sell to us,
the self that burns
with ancient truths,
the self that becomes whole
as it breaks.

what if curiosity was a
birthright,
where knowing yourself
was a revolution?
where loving your neighbor
is not just a command,
it is a way of being?

what if curiosity is a mirror,
reflecting the question:
who am I becoming and
how does my light
spark the light in others?

curious you
by k. buehler

I didn't set out to build a program. I set out to find myself. After years of healing, remembering, reclaiming, and resting, I found myself surrounded by a collection of tools—books, crystals, oils, quotes, scripture, sound bowls, affirmations, astrology charts. Everything I had ever reached for in my search for wholeness, clarity, peace. Yet nothing felt cohesive. It all felt like fragments of a language I hadn't yet learned to speak fluently.

Then came a whisper: "These are the truths my son spoke of. The light within. Heaven within you. If you had faith, you could move mountains. Yet my people can't hear this new sound... not because it isn't true, because it isn't accessible. Translate it. Tell it in a new way."

So I did.

I laid everything out on my desk. My tools. My notes. My tears. My curiosity. I began sorting through the sacred mess. Colors started to emerge —Red, Orange, Yellow, Green, Blue, Indigo, Violet. ROYGBIV. A rainbow. A resonance. A return.

The color spectrum became a framework—not just for energy, for exploration. Not just a system—an invitation. This was the birth of Curious You: PhD in Me™. It wasn't about fixing people. It was about remembering. It was about reclaiming curiosity as a sacred act of self-knowing.

I'll be honest—starting was hard.

I'm someone who loves structure. Who thrives on clarity. I like having the framework and scaffolding before I invite anyone in. The idea of opening something up before it was polished felt vulnerable in ways I wasn't used to.

That's why Brad was such a gift. We were on our way to a board meeting when he said he was starting to believe in something deeper. "Not religion," he said. "Soul-level truth."

I told him about Curious You. And he didn't flinch.

He said, "I'm in."

And he meant it.

He stayed in those early weeks—even when it was chaotic and unpolished. When I was still figuring it out. When I doubted myself. He didn't just stick around—he leaned in.

As a fellow executive and professional, he gave me the gift of presence and perspective. Having someone I respected so deeply walk with me through that ambiguity made me feel seen. Less alone. It validated the vision. And I'll never stop being grateful.

He became the first co-creator—an original Explorer. He became a safe space for me to test out my skills and share what I had learned. We became fast soul-pals.

Then Brad invited Benji—a psychologist and soul-centered human—into the space. And again, I was met with kindness. With curiosity. With resonance. Both of them helped me refine what was possible. They mirrored back to me that this was more than an idea. It was something sacred.

Then came Jen, my acupuncturist and longtime friend. She helped create the essential oil roll-ons and sprays, pairing emotional support with vibrational medicine and ancient wisdom. She matched each blend to a color port, enhancing the emotional frequency of the experience. With her knowledge of traditional and energetic medicine, she brought aroma and resonance into each layer of the journey.

Together—we created. I started naming the pieces.

Synaptexts™ – Soulful nudges and reflective texts, designed to interrupt the noise of daily life with a moment of inner pause. A quote. A question. A prompt to re-engage with yourself. The vulnerability of sending them—to professionals, to peers—was real.

Their responses reminded me: people were hungry for this.

Curiosity Crates™ – Immersive boxes filled with tools for sensory and soul exploration: candles, crystals, tea, oils, tuning forks, bracelets, mini-journals, intention cards. Each one crafted to awaken the senses and stir the spirit.

Soul-u-lar Syntax™ Reports – Personalized astrology reports, interpreted through the lens of color, curiosity, and archetype. They're not just star maps—they're mirrors. Reflections of identity, timing, and resonance. A synthesis of science, poetry, and possibility.

This work—this movement—was never about perfection. It was about presence. About exploration. About reclaiming the parts of ourselves we were taught to hide or ignore.

The deeper I went into Curious You... the more I discovered about me.

When my daughter was diagnosed with dyslexia, something clicked. I saw myself in her—the way she processed, remembered, and responded to information. The frustration with rigidity. The brilliance that didn't always translate on paper.

I realized I had dyslexia, too. It had never been diagnosed. Yet it had always been there. That discovery led me to look even closer. Then something else surfaced—something that finally made everything click.

I have been diagnosed with ADHD for a long time. It's shaped how I move through the world—fast, passionate, full of ideas and interruptions. Even with that awareness, there was still this deeper layer of difference I couldn't quite name.

I always felt like I was on the outside looking in. I felt things more. I noticed things others didn't. I needed structure, scripting, space. Social settings drained me. Emotions flooded me.

I began researching. Reading. Listening to stories of late-diagnosed women. I took assessments—ones designed for adults who had spent a lifetime masking. And the patterns were clear.

I have autism. No doctor handed me a diagnosis, yet my bones knew it was true. It was kind of a relief. I realized I wasn't a defect. It was part of my design.

It was the missing puzzle piece that explained everything: my deep empathy, my intensity, my love for systems, metaphors, and meaning. The way I could sense things before they were spoken. The overwhelm. The shutdowns. The need for recovery after large social gatherings.

In the middle of all that clarity, I discovered something else. I have synesthesia—a neurological trait where the senses intertwine. It means I hear colors. I see sounds. I feel letters. Music has texture. Words have shape. Sometimes, numbers carry emotion. I didn't even know this was different. I just assumed everyone experienced the world this way—through layered frequencies and multi-sensory dimensions.

Apparently, they don't.

Synesthesia is kind of rare and it's often correlated with autism. When I learned that, I exhaled. Not only was I not broken—I was built for resonance. It explained so much.

Why I remember things by color or sensation. Why I understand and process things in pictures. Why I connect so deeply with symbols and rhythm. Why my body sometimes feels what others are too afraid to say. Why sound healing makes so much sense to me. Why I need silence like oxygen.

It's not just that I feel deeply—it's that I experience life as layers of sound, light, and texture. The world is more vivid. And yes, it can be overwhelming. It's also what makes life so beautiful. I realized: I was never too much. I was just tuned differently.

Curious You PhD In Me ™ became the first place I let all of that live out loud. No more masking. No more editing myself into someone else's idea of what "professional" looks like. This was mine. A framework that honors color, texture, intuition, and truth. A place where the way I see and sense the world isn't just allowed—it's useful.

This isn't about labeling. It's about language. It's about giving ourselves a vocabulary for understanding how we move through the world. Because once we understand it, we can navigate it more gracefully. We can stop shrinking and start showing up as we are.

All of this—the autism, the ADHD, the dyslexia, the synesthesia—it isn't a flaw. It's a fingerprint. It's the exact wiring I needed to build this, to hold space, to hear a new sound and translate it.

I've learned so much through this process. About people. About life. About what it means to be fully alive.

Here's what I know now: Most people aren't looking for perfection. They're looking for permission. To show up. To ask questions. To not have it all figured out. To be seen and loved in the in-between. Because life isn't a checklist. It's a conversation. It's a song we're all still writing.

The more curious we become with ourselves, the more compassion we can extend to the world. This is just the beginning. A playground for remembering. A return to the soul of who you've always been. So go ahead—ask the questions.

While I don't have all the answers, I'm finally learning how to live the questions. Maybe that's the whole point. Consider this as your invitation to get a PhD in You.

Seven Souvenirs

You're allowed to ask the questions they told you not to ask. Curiosity is not rebellion. It's remembering. You're not betraying your faith, your family, or your past by wondering who you are beneath the scripts.

Healing doesn't have to look like a spreadsheet or a therapist's couch. Healing might come through colors, music, metaphors, nature, textures, movement or observance. Follow what makes you feel alive. Healing can be sensory, spiritual, and sacred.

You don't need a diagnosis to validate what you know to be true. When you start seeing yourself clearly—your patterns, your processing, your needs—it's okay to claim language that fits, even if there's no official diagnosis. Naming it can help you love it. Understand it. Advocate for it.

Neurodivergence is not the absence of order—it's a different kind of brilliance. Your brain is wired for wonder. For systems. For beauty. For patterns most people miss. You're not too much. You're multidimensional.

Your voice—your way—is a language someone else is waiting to hear. Don't worry about being polished. Be real. Be resonant. People aren't moved by perfection; they're moved by presence.

You're not late to yourself. It doesn't matter if you're discovering this in your 30s, 40s, or beyond. What matters is that you made it. You're here. And every part of your journey was preparation, not detour.

The story doesn't end with the scattering. It begins with the bloom that only grows in the place you once thought was barren.

Purposeful Ponderings

What are you curious about right now—about yourself, your soul, your story?

When was the last time you let yourself play, create, or explore without needing to be "productive"?

Are there parts of you (your brain, your body, your processing style) that you've been taught to hide or shrink? What happens when you begin to accept them?

What labels or diagnoses have helped you make peace with your story? Are there any you've been afraid to explore?

What tools or modalities have you dismissed as "weird" or "woo"—yet felt drawn to? What's stopping you from exploring them?

What would it feel like to give yourself full permission to learn how you work? Not how they told you you should work.

If you were getting a PhD in you, what would your first course be called?

The Promise

not all promises arrive
with clarity or clean lines.
some show up in fragments
a pull in the gut,
a flicker in the dark,
a knowing too big
for language.

i've walked with promises
that changed shape mid-journey
not broken,
just translated
by time,
by growth,
by the deep work of becoming.

some came true
in ways i didn't recognize at first
not as i imagined,
as i needed.
not always loud,
always present.

there were days i mistook
detours for failure,
pauses for the end.
now i know:
purpose doesn't always arrive
on schedule.
it arrives when we're ready
to receive it differently.

i've kept promises
by surrendering to the unfolding.
i've kept them
by changing,
by listening,
by letting go
of what no longer honored
the soul of the vow.

the process is the promise.
the showing up.
the asking.
the returning.
the learning to trust
that even the wandering
has its own kind of precision.

not all fulfillment
looks like a finish line.
sometimes,
it looks like peace.
sometimes,
like alignment.
sometimes,
just like breathing
without bracing anymore.

and maybe
this is the prevailing purpose:
not to keep every promise
the way it was first spoken,
it's to become the version of you
who understands
why it was made.

trust the process
by k. buehler

Becoming a mother was the moment the promise started to look like a person.

Her name is Amelia.

I didn't always want to be a mom. In fact, I swore I wouldn't be. I couldn't bear the thought of a child living through what I did. Of trusting someone to protect their innocence... and watching that trust be shattered.

God had other plans.

When Amelia came into our lives, everything shifted. Not instantly. Not perfectly. Deeply. She cracked open a part of me I didn't know was still buried—the part that longed to feel wonder again. The part that believed in unicorns and magic and dreams that don't make sense to anyone else. She brought color back to the places I had resigned to grayscale.

She made me a mother. And in doing so, she helped me become a child again.

There's something holy about watching your child

laugh in a way you were never allowed to. There's something healing about building a playhouse when you never had one, planning zoo trips, lake adventures, or dressing in matching outfits—not for the photo, for the joy.

There's something transformational about slowing down to watch trains, because she asked you 372 times if today was "October Four." When we finally took her on that train ride, her joy was so full I could barely contain my tears. Because I wasn't just watching her receive a promise—I was watching God remind me that mine are still coming too.

Every bedtime story, every dance party, every "I love you more"—it re-parented something in me. Every giggle was a form of restoration. Every "Mommy, look!" was an invitation to see the world through new eyes.

Motherhood didn't fix me. It freed me.

I used to wonder what life was like for "normal" kids. Treehouses. Family dinners. Parents who loved each other. Photos from every birthday.

And now—I get to be part of that dream. I get to build it. And in doing so, I get to live it too.

This past year I've realized the timing of things doesn't always make sense. Sometimes the promise feels late. Or strange. Or impossible. And what I know now is this: the process is never wasted.

The detours, the delays, the dark nights—they were preparing me. Strengthening me. Refining me. Every setback that looked like failure was actually forming a deeper version of me—the one who could hold the promise when it arrived.

And that promise wasn't just a child. It was a home. A healed nervous system. A self that no longer needs to prove her worth to belong.

The promise is peace. It's presence. It's perspective. It's standing in the kitchen with a dishwasher as your birthday gift and realizing—this is the life I prayed for. And it's good. It's turning 33 and reclaiming the childhood that was stolen, letting magic flood back in through paintbrushes and glitter and butterfly wings.

It's learning that the process was not punishment. It was preparation.

My daughter is now seven. The same age I was when I entered the foster care system. Now, it's time to say something to the girl who started it all.

Dear Seven-Year-Old Me,
I see you. I know what you're carrying—the weight of things a child should never have to bear. I know the fear, the confusion, the way you try to make yourself smaller when you sense the shift in the air, the way you hold your breath, waiting for what's coming next. I know how hard you try to be good, to be perfect, to not give anyone a reason to hurt you. And I know that sometimes, it doesn't matter what you do.

I need you to hear me: None of this is your fault. None of it. The way people treat you is not a reflection of your worth. You are not broken. You are not wrong. You are not here to be anyone's punching bag, secret-keeper, or scapegoat. You are not too much. You are not too loud, too curious, too emotional, or too stubborn. Everything about you that makes people frustrated or uncomfortable will one day be the exact things that make you powerful. Your questions will change lives. Your sensitivity will help others feel seen. Your ability to notice things others miss will guide you to places you never imagined.

I know you think maybe you are in hell. That there's no way this much pain could exist in any other place. I know you wonder if you'll ever escape it, if you'll ever feel safe, if you'll ever be able to breathe without waiting for the next bad thing. I wish I could scoop you up and show you what's coming.

Because one day, you'll have a little girl of your own—a bright, curious, wildly brilliant daughter—and she will look at you with the biggest eyes and ask if she is in heaven. And you will pause, because how could you have ever believed you were in hell when this moment exists?

I won't lie to you—there are hard years ahead. You will learn to survive in ways that later, you will have to unlearn. You will survive. And one day, you will do more than survive. You will heal. You will step into a life that is yours, not the one they tried to force on you. You will use your voice. You will tell your story, and when you do, it will reach others who are still trapped in silence.

I won't ask you to be strong. You shouldn't have to be. I will promise you this: One day, I will come back for you. I will take your hand, and together, we will rewrite the story they tried to write for us. You are worth everything they tried to take from you. You always have been.

And one more thing—never stop writing. Even if you think no one will ever read your words. One day, your words will find their way into the hands of someone who needs them the way you needed them. One day, your words will be the proof that you made it out. That you didn't just survive—you built a beautiful life where love thrives.

I love you. I believe in you. I am you.

With all the love you should have had,
Your Future Self

Seven Souvenirs

The promise doesn't always arrive in the package you expected. Sometimes it looks like a train ride with a three-year-old. Sometimes it sounds like belly laughs in the kitchen. Sometimes it feels like breathing without fear. Stay open—it might surprise you.

The process is sacred, even when it's messy. Growth doesn't always feel good. Healing isn't always gentle. Even in the ache, there is holy ground being formed beneath your feet.

What broke you may have been part of building you. That doesn't mean it was okay. It means you alchemized it. You transmuted the pain into purpose, the wounds into wisdom, the survival into strength.

You are allowed to rewrite your legacy. You are not destined to repeat cycles. You are not obligated to carry the burdens your parents never laid down. You can love your child without reliving your childhood. You can become the ancestor who changed everything.

Healing happens in the ordinary moments. In playhouses and dance parties. In mismatched pajamas and bedtime books. In apologizing when you get it wrong. In laughing so hard you cry. In choosing presence over perfection.

The promise is not a destination—it's a way of being. It's peace, not performance. It's truth, not titles. It's joy that doesn't demand explanation. It's living rooted in your full, radiant, unapologetic self.

You are the promise. Your life. Your light. Your presence. Your healing. You are living proof that the story can change. That love wins. That broken things can bloom again.

Purposeful Ponderings

When you think about "the promise," what does that look or feel like in your life? What were you hoping for —and what did it teach you?

What parts of the process do you find yourself resisting? Can you explore why?

What would happen if you softened into the unfolding?

Are there cycles you've already broken that you haven't celebrated yet? Take a moment to acknowledge the promises already in motion.

How has parenting (or re-parenting yourself) taught you what love really is?

What has your child (or your inner child) taught you about wonder, play, and truth?

In what ways have you rewritten the story you were handed? What story are you creating now?

If you could go back and whisper something to your younger self, what would it be?

Healing Resources

If you're here, it's because something in these pages touched something tender in you. Maybe it stirred a memory, named an ache, or lit a small spark of possibility.

You are not alone. You are not to blame. You are worthy of healing, support, and peace—no matter how long it's been or how deep it goes. Below are trusted organizations, communities, and offerings. Take what you need, leave what you don't.

Resource	Focus Area	Contact
RAINN (Rape, Abuse & Incest National Network)	Crisis support and resources for survivors of sexual violence	www.rainn.org
National Sexual Violence Resource Center	Education, advocacy, and resources to prevent and respond to sexual violence	www.nsvrc.org
1in6	Support for male survivors of sexual abuse	1in6.org
Handing the Shame Back	Global support for adult survivors of child sexual abuse	www.handingtheshameback.org/
Stop It Now!	Prevention and support around child sexual abuse and exploitation	www.stopitnow.org
National Center for Missing & Exploited Children (NCMEC)	Support for victims of child sexual abuse material (CSAM)	www.missingkids.org
What Happened to You? by Dr. Bruce Perry & Oprah Winfrey	Explores childhood trauma, brain development, and resilience	www.oprah.com/what-happened-to-you-book

About The Author

k. buehler is the pen name of Krista Tedrow—a poet, publisher, and story steward who writes from the sacred space where healing meets honesty. Her words hold a frequency of remembrance, written for those learning to live, love, and lead from their innermost truth.

Krista chose to write under the name k. buehler as an act of reclamation. After a childhood marked by loss, silence, and survival, she returned to her birth name not as a wound—as a witness. A way to say: This is where I come from. And this is who I choose to become.

She is the founder and publisher of NOW LLC, a home for books that carry soul and spark, and a consulting firm that goes by the same name. She works with a rural non-profit writing grants, designing healing-centered programs, and launching innovative pilot projects that center equity, belonging, and lived experience.

Krista is the founder and creator of Curious You: PhD in Me™, an experiential framework that invites people to explore who they are beneath the roles they've performed. Through color, astrology, neuroscience, sound, and story, it offers a gentle yet radical path to self-remembrance.

She lives in southern Iowa where her daughter Amelia teaches her how to see the world with wonder and reminds her daily that becoming is a lifelong poem.

Made in the USA
Monee, IL
18 June 2025